LOTS OF THINGS
TO KNOW ABOUT
YOUR BODY

Sarah Hull

Illustrated by
Susanna Rumiz

Designed by
Katie Webb

With expert advice from Doctor Salma Ahmed

USBORNE QUICKLINKS

For links to websites where you can watch videos, try quizzes and find even **more** facts about the human body, go to **usborne.com/Quicklinks** and type in the title of this book.

Please follow the internet safety guidelines at Usborne Quicklinks. Children should be supervised online.

Did you know that your skin is your body's biggest organ?

Amazing! But what is an organ?

You can check the meaning of that word in the glossary on page 62. And there's an index on pages 63-64 to help you search for a topic.

Take a deep breath

Can you feel your chest move out?
Air is rushing into your lungs...

The air blows up
600,000,000 tiny
balloons called alveoli.

ALVEOLI

This is how your
body gets oxygen
from the air.
You need oxygen
to stay alive.

Usually, you do this
about 16 times every
minute — without
thinking about it.

You can probably hold
your breath for about
30 seconds to a minute.

But some trained divers can
hold their breath for as long as
20 minutes.

3

Why do you have a belly button?

Your belly button just sits on your tummy, but once upon a time, it **kept you alive**.

Before you were born, you grew for about 9 months inside a warm and cosy womb.

Back then, your belly button was a tube called the umbilical cord.

WOMB

UMBILICAL CORD

It brought you food, water and oxygen — everything you needed to grow and stay alive.

After you were born, the tube dried up and fell off, but it left a mark behind — your belly button.

Does your belly button stick out, or does it go in?

Babies are WEIRDER than you think...

Babies grow moustaches while they're still in the womb.

The hair is called **lanugo**. When babies have been growing for about four months, it appears on the upper lip, then spreads over the rest of their bodies.

Lanugo usually drops off before the baby is born.

Newborn babies can't cry properly. They make the right noises, but their eyes don't make any tears!

Waaaaaaaaaahh!

It takes about a **month** before a baby's eyes start making tears.

Babies have more bones than you do. Their skeletons have around **300** parts. But as they grow, their bones become harder and some of them join together.

Four bones in the top of the skull join to make one.

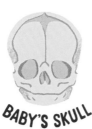

BABY'S SKULL

ADULT'S SKULL

By the time you're fully grown, you'll have around **206** bones.

You'll never guess how much you'll eat

Food and drink are the fuel that keeps your body going.
Over your entire life, you'll need **a lot**.

You'll probably eat food weighing more than **five elephants!**

You'll drink enough to fill at least **six concrete mixer trucks.**

Inside your tummy...

...there's a chemical called **hydrochloric acid**. In large amounts, it would be powerful enough to dissolve metal.

This acid is in juices in your stomach. It helps break down tough food, so your body can get the energy out of it.

SALAD

BREAD CRUST

APPLE

FIZZZ...

We're melting!

STOMACH

It also kills germs in food that could make you ill.

POP!

STOMACH JUICES

Why doesn't the acid dissolve my tummy?

MUCUS

Ah. That's because slimy mucus lines your tummy, protecting it from the acid.

7

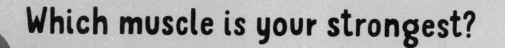

Which muscle is your strongest?

The **hardest-working** muscle in your body is your heart.

It started pumping blood about 8 months before you were born and won't stop until the day you die.

The muscles in the back of your lower legs are **very strong**.

They pull to keep your body upright and help you stand on tip-toe.

The **biggest** muscles in your body are in your bottom.

They help you stand up after sitting or crouching down.

Excuse me!

Watch out, it's about to get a little smelly over here...

Farts are a bit rude, but they're completely normal and healthy.

Oops!

Everyone farts around 5—15 times a day...

parp!

...releasing about enough gas to fill a **party balloon**.

How much time you'll spend on the toilet

All different shapes and sizes

See how the tallest and smallest people ever measure up to an ordinary bed.

Most people fit comfortably in a standard bed...

...but it would have been **far** too short for Robert Pershing Wadlow, one of the tallest people ever to have lived.

I'm the same height as Chandra Bahadur Dangi, the shortest adult ever.

1.6m
(5ft 3in)

54.6cm
(1ft 9½in)

2.72m
(8ft 11in)

Some measurements are the same for **everyone**, whatever size or shape they are.

Spread your arms as wide as they go.

The distance between your fingertips...

...is usually the same as from the top of your head to the soles of your feet.

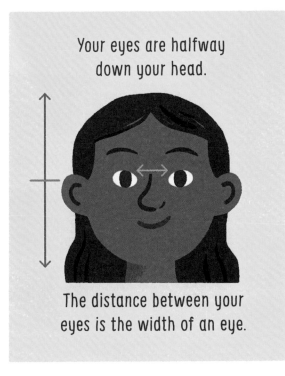

Your eyes are halfway down your head.

The distance between your eyes is the width of an eye.

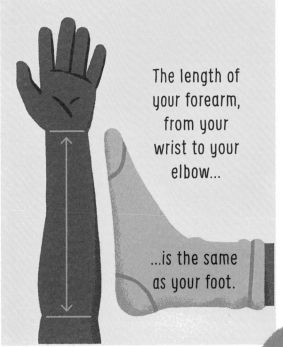

The length of your forearm, from your wrist to your elbow...

...is the same as your foot.

13

One-of-a-kind prints

Look closely at the ends of your fingers and you'll see patterns of loops, whorls or arches.

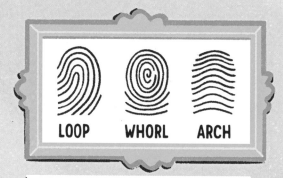

LOOP   WHORL   ARCH

Unknown artist's fingerprints

No one in the whole world has the same fingerprint patterns as you.

Max's right-hand prints

Milo's right-hand prints

Not even identical twins have the same fingerprints.

Guess what! If you could take a print from your tongue, it would be different from everyone else's too.

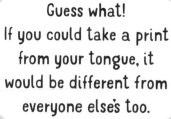

MAX

MILO

CRIME SCENE

Whenever you touch something, you leave behind faint fingerprints. Fingerprints can help detectives solve a crime.

The only thing the robber took was a eucalyptus plant.

Detectives just have to find someone whose fingerprints match the ones at the scene of a crime.

But maybe detectives shouldn't be looking for a human at all...

It turns out that koala and chimpanzee fingerprints look almost exactly the same as human ones.

It wasn't ME!

You're electric!

There's electricity whizzing around your body all the time. It's used to carry messages to and from the brain.

When you touch something, an electrical message is sent from your fingertips to your brain.

Fluffy!

PING!

CUDDLE IT!

Messages zoom along **really fast** — they're the fastest thing in your body.

PING!

PING!

CUDDLE IT!

Your tongue only knows five tastes

Broccoli, raspberries, chocolate cake and cheese...
These foods are **very** different, but to your tongue,
they're all a mix of just five tastes.

Hello, we're tiny sensors on your tongue called TASTE BUDS. You have thousands of us.

SWEET

SOUR

BITTER

SALTY

UMAMI

The fifth taste is called UMAMI. It's a savoury flavour.

Each taste bud tests for one of the five tastes.

But your taste buds aren't the only things at work when you eat...

That LOOKS good and it SMELLS so chocolatey!

Mmm... so gooey!

Squiiish

Your nose, eyes and mouth work **together** to build up a much fuller picture of what foods are like.

Why Brussels sprouts are yucky

Children are **supertasters**. They have a whopping **30,000** taste buds in their mouths.

All these taste buds make children especially sensitive to bitter tastes — like the ones in Brussels sprouts.

A little bitterness can be yummy, but a lot is disgusting.

BITTER

Ugh, Brussels sprouts are yucky!

No, they're delicious!

Grown-ups only have around **10,000** taste buds, so Brussels sprouts don't taste as bitter to them.

Your height changes even when you're fully grown

When you wake up in the morning, you're actually taller than when you went to bed.

You're taller!

THIS MORNING
LAST NIGHT

About this much taller for grown-ups.

0 inches
0 cm 1
2
3
1

During the day, you're on your feet a lot, carrying the weight of your body — and sometimes even more.

Waaah!

WOOF, WOOF!

That weight squashes the knobbly bones in your back and the bones in your knees closer together.

At night, when you lie down, they stretch out again.

Aaaahh!

Space travel makes you taller

In space, your body is almost weightless, so the bones in your back and legs don't get squashed together **at all**. In fact, these bones get further apart.

Astronauts can grow this much taller in space!

0 inches
0 cm 1
2
3
4
5
1
2

After a few months back down on Earth, our heights return to normal.

Why your blood is red

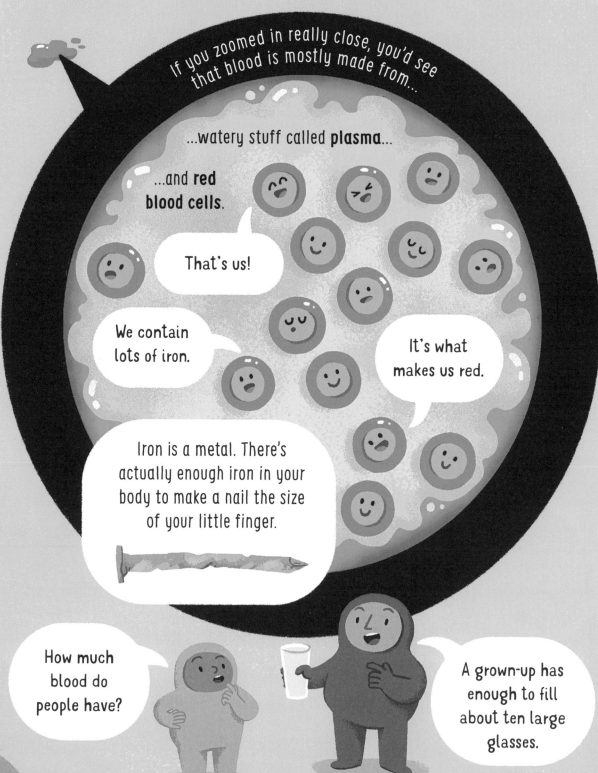

Ba-bump, ba-bump, ba-bump...

Your heart is a muscle. It's about the size of your fist, but it pumps blood **all around** your body, keeping you alive.

BRAIN THIS WAY

Blood flows to every part of your body through tiny tubes.

ba-bump...

FROM THE LUNGS

TO THE LUNGS

Your heart pumps blood to your lungs to pick up oxygen.

Then red blood cells deliver oxygen around your body...

...before heading back to your heart to start again.

BACK TO THE HEART

Whoooooooh

It takes just **one minute** for blood to travel all around your body and back to your heart.

DOWN TO THE TOES

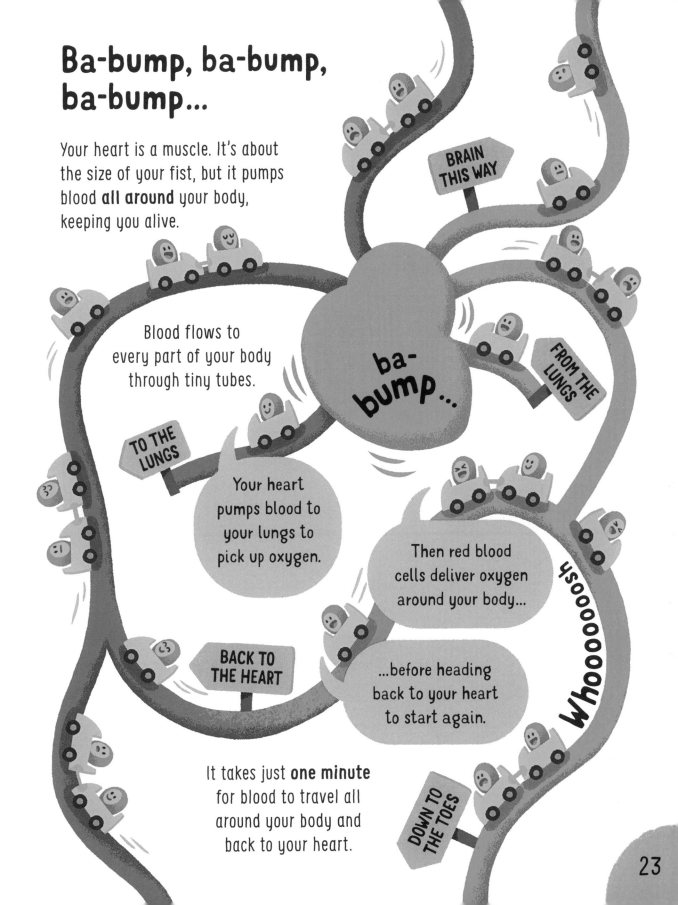

Every body needs help with something

The way people's bodies look and work can be very different. Some differences are more obvious than others, but everyone has different strengths and different things they need help with.

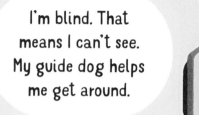

I'm blind. That means I can't see. My guide dog helps me get around.

Lots of people need to wear glasses or contact lenses to see clearly — about three people in every four.

Beep beep!

I find it difficult to speak, so I'm using sign language to talk to my friend instead.

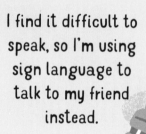

I wear a hearing aid to help me to hear.

Someone who's shy might find it hard to talk to people.

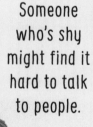

Hi!

Vital organs?

Your body has lots of different parts called organs that work together to keep you alive. But you **don't** actually need them all...

So how come not all organs are vital?

At the back of your mouth, are two bumps — your **tonsils**. They're part of how your body fights off germs, but you don't need them.

People's tonsils are sometimes removed, if they keep getting infected.

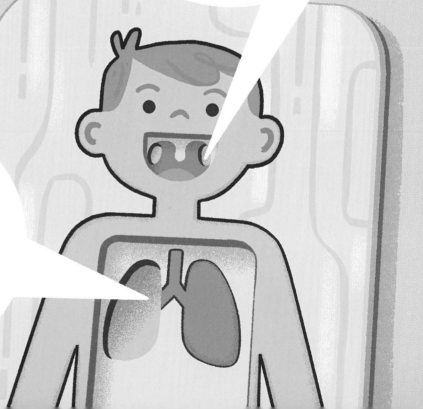

Two **lungs** inside your chest breathe for you. But you can survive with one.

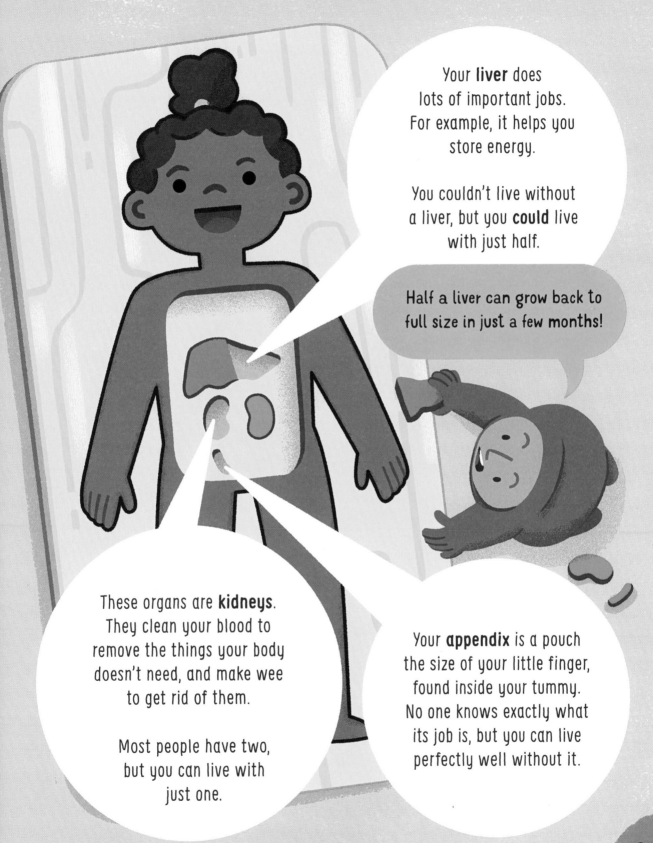

Your **liver** does lots of important jobs. For example, it helps you store energy.

You couldn't live without a liver, but you **could** live with just half.

Half a liver can grow back to full size in just a few **months**!

These organs are **kidneys**. They clean your blood to remove the things your body doesn't need, and make wee to get rid of them.

Most people have two, but you can live with just one.

Your **appendix** is a pouch the size of your little finger, found inside your tummy. No one knows exactly what its job is, but you can live perfectly well without it.

When dust or dirt tickles inside your nose or throat, you might need to sneeze.

A sneeze is an **explosion** of air that sends tiny drops of water and snot flying out of your nose and mouth.

Ahh-choooooooo!

Sneezes burst out at an incredible speed and can travel as far as the length of a bus.

Inside sneeze droplets are extremely small things called germs – like me.

There are THOUSANDS of germs in every sneeze.

We can make you ill.

Yuck! Next time, try to trap it in a tissue.

A LOT of snot

If thinking about snot makes you turn a little... green, **turn the page now!**

Your nose makes a **lot** of snot. But only a **small** amount of it comes out of your nostrils.

Most snot runs down the back of your nose and into your tummy!

Eugh!

I'm stuck!

All this snot is there to trap germs and dirt you breathe in, so they can't cause any problems.

You swallow about one stomach-full of snot every day. The germs get killed in your stomach.

TO THE STOMACH ↓

29

Drink up!

More than half of your body is actually **water**.

Drinking at least six glasses of water every day keeps your body's water supplies topped up.

Your body loses water every day, when you sweat, when you breathe out, and when you go to the toilet.

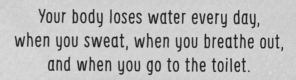

In hot weather, you can sweat as much as two large glasses of water every hour!

If your body was a bottle, it'd be filled to about here with water.
↓

If you lose more water than you drink, your brain finds it harder to think clearly and your body starts feeling tired. You might even faint.

Water's best, but you can get a lot of water by drinking juice and milk too.

People can only survive for a few days without drinking.

You couldn't live without...

Your body needs all sorts of chemicals to survive. Luckily, your body can get them in just the right amounts from ordinary foods.

Stay healthy with ZINC

Your body needs **zinc** to help fight off germs that cause diseases.

Beans

Eat IRON

Without **iron**, your body couldn't make blood.

Beans

Lentils

Dried apricots

Potassium helps your muscles, including your heart. Without it, things would soon go wrong.

Rich in MAGNESIUM

Your body needs **magnesium** and **calcium** to build strong bones and teeth.

Seeds

POTASSIUM-rich foods here

High in CALCIUM

Bodies worth MILLIONS!

Some people have special talents that rely on a particular part of their body. A few insure these parts for **vast** sums of money.

What does insuring part of your body mean?

Well... if that part was injured, the owner would receive lots of money. Here are some of the amazing body parts that famous people have insured.

FEET

Dancer Michael Flatley's astounding feet set a world record for tap dancing, tapping 35 times in just one second!

TIPPITY

TAPPITY

TAP

VOICE

Singer Mariah Carey's incredible voice can sing a far wider range of notes than most singers.

I don't want a lot for Christmas...

LEGS

Footballer Cristiano Ronaldo's legs have scored well over 750 goals, helping his team to victory.

THWUMP!

€€€

TASTE BUDS

£££

Hayleigh Curtis is a **chocolate scientist**. Her extra-ordinary taste buds help her invent delicious new types of chocolate.

Mmm... it's got that melt-in-the-mouth texture, but it's a little too sweet.

HANDS

Star pianist Lang Lang's hands dance across the piano keys, making magnificent music.

PLINKITY   TINKLY   PLINK $$$

33

You'll never guess who's hairier

A chimpanzee **looks** a lot hairier than a human...

....but humans actually have just as much hair as chimpanzees. It's just that most human hairs are much finer and shorter.

I'm bald, so I can't be as hairy as a chimpanzee.

You are – even bald heads have hair. It's just so short and fine you can barely see it.

The only places your skin is **truly** bald are your lips and the palms of your hands and the soles of your feet.

When it comes to the number of hairs on their heads, some people have more than others.

Redheads have the **fewest** hairs — around 90,000.

People with black hair have about 100,000.

If you have brown hair, you probably have around 110,000.

People with blond hair have the **most** — about 120,000.

Hair is made of strong, stretchy stuff called **keratin**.

All these things are made of keratin too.

FINGERNAILS

CLAWS

HORNS

HOOVES

Around and around the world...

During your life, you'll walk, run or roll a really long way — far enough to take you **three times** around the world.

That's around 170 million steps!

Every step you take uses around 200 muscles.

You'll go EVEN FURTHER if you do lots of sport!

Which is more tiring, standing or walking?

Whether you're walking, dancing or standing still, strong stretchy muscles under your skin are **always working**.

Walking uses **all** the muscles in your legs and feet, but not at the same time. That means they share the work.

I could **march** like this for **hours**.

I've only been **standing** for 10 minutes and **my legs** are already tired.

When you stand still, some muscles in your feet, legs and back have to work to keep you in position. They don't get any breaks, so can quickly start to ache.

So standing might not look as energetic as walking, but it's actually more tiring.

You're a lot like everyone else...

Every single part of you is built following
a set of **instructions** called **DNA**.
There's DNA everywhere inside your body.

DNA

Your DNA tells your body
how tall it should grow.

Your DNA decides
whether your hair is
curly or straight.

Your DNA is the reason
your eyes are brown or
blue or green.

Humans all look **really** different, but when it comes
to their DNA, they're almost exactly the same.

This blue part shows
how much DNA you share
with everyone.

Just this tiny red part is different.
It's what makes you **you**.

...and you're *quite* like a banana

It's not just humans that are built according to DNA instructions.
Every living thing is — from mice and jellyfish, to bananas.

Guess what! Lots of these DNA instructions are the same, whether you're a human, a mouse or a banana.

Only this much DNA makes us different!

You share this much DNA with a mouse.

←————————————————→

You share this much DNA with a jellyfish.

←————————→

And you share this much DNA with a banana!

←——→

Remember, remember...

Your brain is about the size of two clenched fists, but it can hold an enormous amount of information.

It has enough memory power to store as much as...

...four billion books...

That's far more books than have ever been published!

How your ears help you balance

Ears help you hear, but they also have another important job...

Deep inside each ear there's a strange tube with three loops that helps you **balance**.

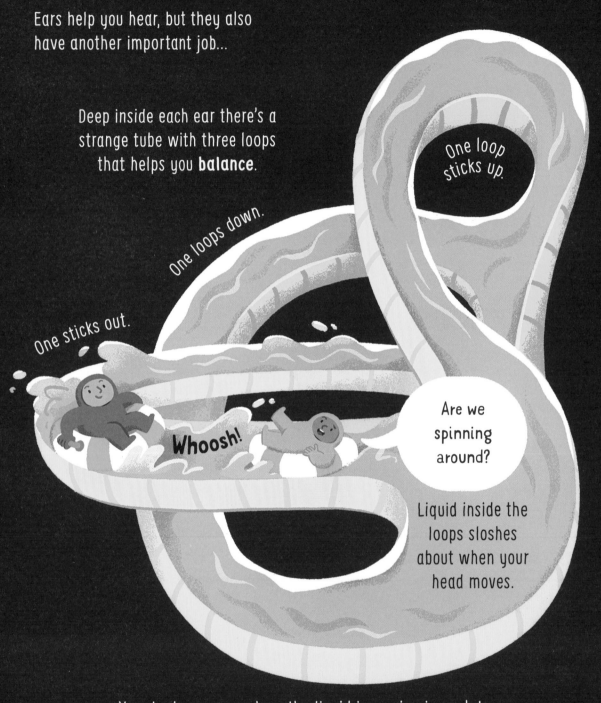

One loop sticks up.

One loops down.

One sticks out.

Whoosh!

Are we spinning around?

Liquid inside the loops sloshes about when your head moves.

Your brain measures how the liquid is moving in each loop.
This allows it to keep track of what's up and down, and left and right,
and helps you to keep your balance.

Have you ever spun around and around?

Wheeee!

I'm so DIZZY!

The liquid in your ears keeps moving for a while after you've stopped spinning. This confuses your sense of what's up and down, right and left.

If the loops in your ears didn't work properly, you would feel like this **all** the time.

You'd probably fall over a lot.

You'd feel dizzy all the time.

And you definitely wouldn't be able to balance on one leg.

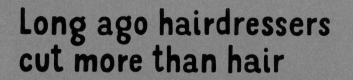

Long ago hairdressers cut more than hair

Barbers used to do **surgery** as well as haircuts and shaves.

Europe, 700 years ago...

What can I do for you? Do you need an arm chopped off? Or perhaps you'd like a tooth out?

Argh, no! Just a shave, please.

Back then, surgery was very risky. Many patients didn't survive.

There was no way of numbing pain, so surgery hurt a lot, too.

How long a beard can grow

Beard hairs grow faster than all other human hairs.

In ancient Egypt, beards were a way of showing how important you were. Kings often wore fake beards made of metal. Sometimes queens did too!

If a man never trimmed his beard...

...it would grow as long as **five times** his height in his lifetime.

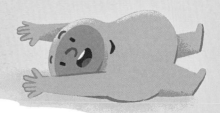

What's eating your lunch

Inside your tummy there are trillions of tiny living things called bacteria. It might sound icky, but you **need** them!

We bacteria help you DIGEST your food.

That means we break it down to get out the things that give you energy and help you grow.

We get good stuff called vitamins out of fruit and vegetables for you.

I'm good at digesting meat.

Unfortunately, some of these bacteria also make smelly gas.

TOILETS

Everything your body **doesn't** need from food comes out as poo.

Rumbling tummies

Did you know doctors call tummy rumbles **borborygmi** (bore-bore-IG-me)?

These rumbles are the sound of food, stomach juices and gas as they move through the tubes in your tummy.

Gurrrgle rrrumble

Hmm... sounds hungry to me!

A full tummy muffles the noises. If you're hungry and your tummy's empty, rumbles can be **much** louder.

Can you guess what these medical names describe?

SYNCHRONOUS DIAPHRAGMATIC FLUTTER

HIC...
HIC...
HIC...

Hiccups

HORRIPILATION

Goosebumps

SPHENOPALATINE GANGLIONEURALGIA

Brain freeze

Your bones are alive

The bones in museums are old and dry. They're very different from the ones living inside your body.

Those bones look like stones!

Dinosaur bones are SO old that they've become stones called fossils... They're not like YOURS at all.

The outsides of your bones are **really** hard.

Inside, there are lots of **holes**.

This makes your bones strong enough to hold you up, but light enough to carry around.

The holes are filled with a liquid called **bone marrow**. Your blood is made in your bone marrow.

Tiny tubes carry the blood out of your bones and around your body.

Funny bones

X-ray machines can show the bones inside your body. They make black and white pictures like the ones on these pages.

These are the **smallest** bones in your body. They're actually the size shown here.

They're hidden deep inside your ears. They vibrate to **help you hear**.

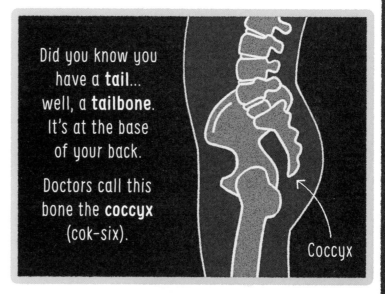

Did you know you have a **tail**... well, a **tailbone**. It's at the base of your back.

Doctors call this bone the **coccyx** (cok-six).

Coccyx

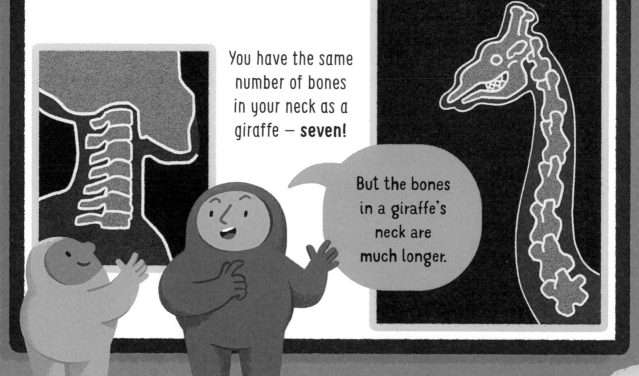

You have the same number of bones in your neck as a giraffe — **seven!**

But the bones in a giraffe's neck are much longer.

What's that smell?

Scientists think your nose can tell apart at least a **trillion** different smells — that's **1,000,000,000,000!**

Smells help you enjoy food. Most of how food **tastes** is actually down to how it **smells**.

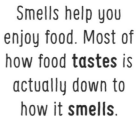

Smells can warn you of **dangers**, such as fire or rotten food that could make you sick.

Your nose can even help you predict the weather.

That earthy smell means a storm is approaching!

Your **body** produces all kinds of smells.

You might notice your body smells different if you eat smelly foods, or haven't washed for a while.

People's smells can change slightly when they are unwell. Humans can't usually detect these smells, but sometimes dogs can...

Dogs' noses can be trained to sniff out diseases.

BLOOD SAMPLES

A
B
C

My human smells a little different before she gets a bad headache.

My nose can sniff out cancer.

I make sure she knows to take medicine, so she won't feel as ill.

What's the time?

Even if you don't know what time it is, your body does. Part of your brain is always keeping time for you. It's known as your **body clock**.

Your body clock controls chemicals called **hormones**. These are sent around your body at different times of the day to tell your body what to do.

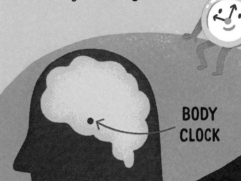

BODY CLOCK

In the morning, your body clock lets your body know it's time to wake up.

DRRRR...

It lets you know it's time to eat...

...and when you have energy to work and play.

When it's time to sleep, your body clock slows down your body, so it can rest.

That's why you can feel so groggy and awful if you're awake when you should be asleep.

But HOW does my body clock know what time it is?

Light. Your eyes detect the cycle of day and night, and set your body clock to match it.

That's why you shouldn't look at screens before bed. Their light can confuse your body clock and make it harder to fall asleep.

OUCH!

Sometimes the place where you feel pain isn't the part that's actually hurt.

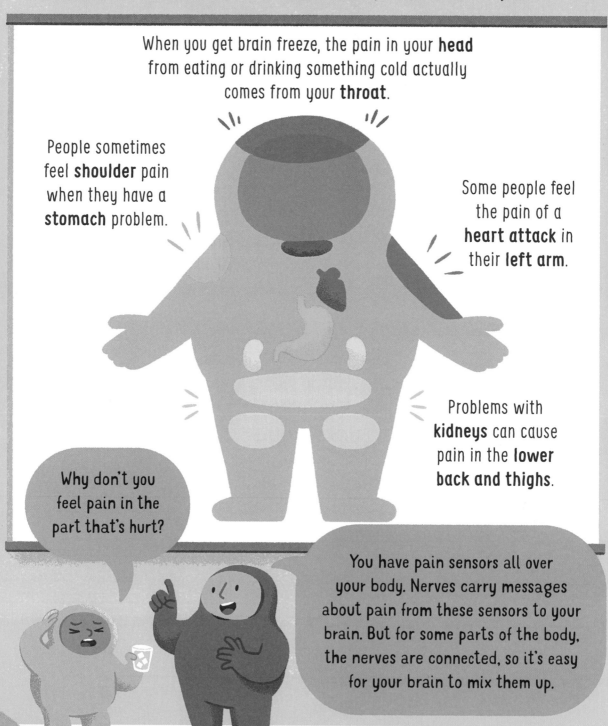

When you get brain freeze, the pain in your **head** from eating or drinking something cold actually comes from your **throat**.

People sometimes feel **shoulder** pain when they have a **stomach** problem.

Some people feel the pain of a **heart attack** in their **left arm**.

Problems with **kidneys** can cause pain in the **lower back and thighs**.

Why don't you feel pain in the part that's hurt?

You have pain sensors all over your body. Nerves carry messages about pain from these sensors to your brain. But for some parts of the body, the nerves are connected, so it's easy for your brain to mix them up.

Your brain can't hurt

The only part of your body that doesn't have pain sensors is your **brain**.

Normally, patients are put to sleep before an operation, so they don't feel any pain. But a patient can be kept awake during brain surgery and not feel a thing.

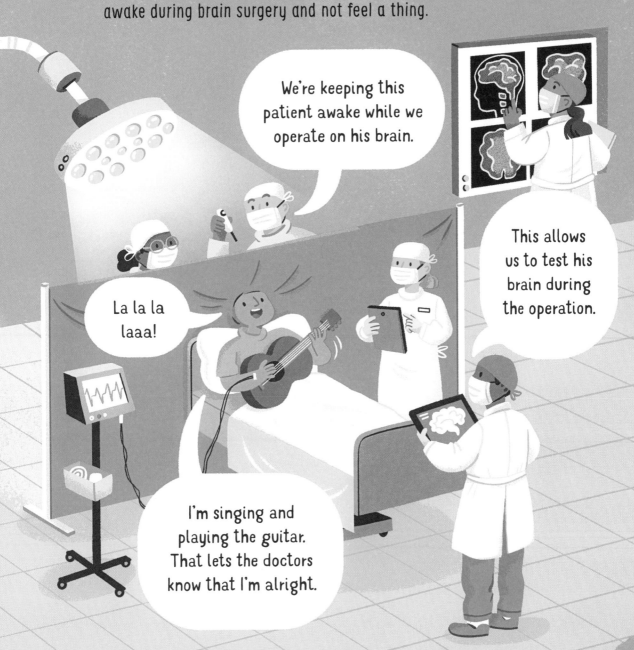

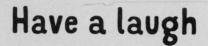

Have a laugh

There are lots of reasons to have a giggle...
but did you know that smiling and laughing
are actually **good** for you?

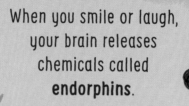

When you smile or laugh,
your brain releases
chemicals called
endorphins.

Endorphins make you
feel good. They can
even reduce feelings
of pain.

Smiling and laughing
can bring you **closer
to friends** or even help
you make new ones.

A proper belly laugh is good
exercise for muscles in your
chest, tummy and shoulders,
as well as your heart.

So, after a belly
laugh, these muscles
feel more **relaxed**.

The tiniest things can hurt your body the most

Germs are tiny — **far** too small to see — but if they get inside your body, they can make you ill. Here are some common germs...

SARS-COV-2
Disease: **COVID-19**

I was discovered in December 2019.

VARICELLA-ZOSTER VIRUS
Disease: **CHICKENPOX**

We've got NOTHING to do with chicken!

We cause itchy red spots.

INFLUENZA VIRUS
Disease: **FLU**

STREPTOCOCCUS MUTANS
Disease: **TOOTH DECAY**

We live on your teeth. Acid we make can damage them.

Loves: sugary foods

Hates: teeth-brushing

CAMPYLOBACTER
Disease: **FOOD POISONING**

I can give you a sore tummy and diarrhoea.

Loves: raw meat

Hates: being cooked

How your body fights germs

Luckily, your body has its own tiny germ-fighting squad to stop germs from making you ill...

Meet the **white blood cells**.

We travel all around your body, fighting germs.

Some of us attack germs with weapons called antibodies.

ANTIBODY

Some of us gobble germs up...

Burp!

When the germs are dead, you feel better again.

You're about to yawn...

You've probably caught a cold or a cough from someone before, but did you know that you can catch a yawn?

Seeing someone yawn, **reading** the word "yawn" or even just **thinking** about yawning can make you need to...

There are scientific experiments that show you're even **more** likely to catch a yawn if you're told **not** to yawn.

Some people catch yawns more easily than others. Did you make it to the bottom of this page without yawning, or wanting to yawn?

While you're dreaming

You may be asleep when you dream, but your **brain** is hard at work.

It reminds itself about things you've learned during the day.

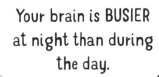

Your brain is BUSIER at night than during the day.

Pamplemousse

FRENCH DICTIONARY

Your brain also files memories away...

Fun at school

SCARY

Me & Teddy

EXIT

And it flushes out waste that collects in your brain while you're awake.

All this helps you stay happy, healthy and ready to learn new things.

Glossary

alveoli — tiny balloon-like parts of your **lungs** that fill with air when you breathe

appendix — a pouch inside your tummy the size of your little finger

bacteria — tiny living things, some are good and some are **germs**

brain — a squishy **organ** in your head that controls almost everything you do

disability — a condition of the body or mind that makes it more difficult for someone to do certain things

DNA — a set of instructions, found everywhere in your body, that decides how your body looks and works

germs — tiny things — some alive, some not — that can make you ill

heart — an **organ** made from **muscle** that pumps blood around your body

heart attack — when someone's **heart** stops working properly

hormones — chemicals released by your body that tell it what to do

kidneys — two **organs** in your lower back that clean your blood and make wee

liver — an **organ** that does lots of important jobs, such as storing energy and releasing **hormones**

lungs — two **organs** in your chest that breathe for you

mucus — slimy snotty watery stuff inside your nose and other **organs**

muscle — a body part used for moving

nerves — thread-like things that carry messages from your body to your **brain** and from your brain to your body

operation — when doctors cut open the body to make repairs inside

organ — a part of your body that does a particular set of jobs

oxygen — a gas in the air that you need to breathe to stay alive

red blood cells — tiny round red blobs in your blood that deliver oxygen around your body

stomach — an **organ** in your tummy that holds food after you swallow it

surgery — see **operation**

taste buds — tiny little bumps on your tongue that help you taste food

tonsils — two small **organs** at the back of your mouth, that are part of how your body fights germs

umbilical cord — a tube that brings food, water and **oxygen** to babies while they grow in the **womb**

womb — an **organ** where babies grow before they are born

Index

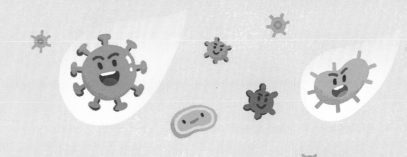

Series editor: Ruth Brocklehurst
Series designer: Stephen Moncrieff

First published in 2022 by Usborne Publishing Ltd., 83-85 Saffron Hill, London EC1N 8RT,
United Kingdom. usborne.com Copyright © 2022 Usborne Publishing Ltd. The name Usborne
and the Balloon logo are Trademarks of Usborne Publishing Ltd. All rights reserved. No part
of this publication may be reproduced, stored in any retrievable system, or transmitted in
any form or by any means, without the prior permission of the publisher. UKE.

Usborne Publishing is not responsible and does not accept liability for the availability
or content of any website other than its own, or for any exposure to harmful, offensive
or inaccurate material which may appear on the Web. Usborne Publishing will have no
liability for any damage or loss caused by viruses that may be downloaded as a
result of browsing the sites it recommends.